THE HIGHEST HEAVEN

A Full-length Play

by

JOSE CRUZ GONZALEZ

Dramatic Publishing
Woodstock, Illinois • England • Australia • New Zealand

*** NOTICE ***

"When we are really honest with ourselves we must admit that our lives are all that really belong to us. So, it is how we use our lives that determines what kind of men we are. It is my deepest belief that only by giving our lives do we find life."

—César Chávez

"La necesidad desconoce fronteras."
"Necessity knows no borders."

—Mexican American Proverb

"Butterflies
Flying Like the Breeze
Sucking Nectar Quietly
Colors Everywhere"

—Kelsey Miguel González, Age 9

"If you haven't forgiven yourself something, how can you forgive others?"

—Dolores Huerta

IMPORTANT BILLING AND CREDIT REQUIREMENTS

All producers of the play *must* give credit to the author(s) of the play in all programs distributed in connection with performances of the play and in all instances in which the title of the play appears for purposes of advertising, publicizing or otherwise exploiting the play and/or a production. The name of the author(s) *must* also appear on a separate line, on which no other name appears, immediately following the title, and *must* appear in size of type not less than fifty percent the size of the title type. Biographical information on the author(s), if included in this book, may be used on all programs. *On all programs this notice must appear:*

"Produced by special arrangement with
THE DRAMATIC PUBLISHING COMPANY of Woodstock, Illinois"

The Highest Heaven premiered with Childsplay, Inc., in association with Borderlands Theater in January 1999 at the Tucson Center for the Performing Arts and February 1999 at the Tempe Performing Arts Center, Tempe, Arizona.

CAST

Huracán .... STEVEN PENA
Kika/Wife......................... ALEJANDRA GARCIA
El Negro.............................. ELLEN BENTON
Doña Elena......................... DEBRA K. STEVENS
Moises, Police Official, Addict, Undertaker-Barber, Husband...
JON GENTRY

PRODUCTION STAFF

Director .... DAVID SAAR
Scenic Design............................ GRO JOHRE
Costume Design......................... CONNIE FURR
Lighting Design .... AMARANTE LUCERO
Music Composition/Sound Design. . RICK ARECCO & ALLEN LEA
Dramaturg .... GRAHAM WHITEHEAD
Properties .... DARREN GOAD
Technical Director .... KENNETH P. LAGER JR.
Stage Manager .... MARIE KRUEGER-JONES

Originally developed at Childsplay, Inc. with support from the NEA/TCG Theatre Residency Program for Playwrights.

The Highest Heaven was workshopped in 1996 at the New Visions/New Voices Program, The Kennedy Center, Washington, D.C.

Special thanks: David Saar, Debra K. Stevens, Graham Whitehead, Rosemary Walsh, Childsplay, NEA/TCG, The Kennedy Center's New Visions/New Voices Program, John McCluggage, Mary Hall Surface, Susan Mason, Palabras, the San Jose Repertory, CSULA, Isaiah Sanders, Lucille Oliver, Alejandra Garcia Iñiguez, and my family.

The Highest Heaven received its second production with the Center Theatre Group/Mark Taper Forum's P.L.A.Y., Los Angeles, Calif., February 7-March 4, 2000.

CAST

Doña Elena, Kika, Wife............... CHRISTINE DEAVER
Moises, Police Official, Addict, Undertaker-Barber...........
                                       DAVID FURUMOTO
Huracán .... OMAR GOMEZ
El Negro............................ RICKE V. HOWELL

PRODUCTION STAFF and CREW

Director .... DIANE RODRIGUEZ
Set Design .... EDWARD E. HAYNES JR.
Costume Design........................ INGRID FERRIN
Lighting Design .... JOSE LOPEZ
Musical Director/Sound Design........... DAVE OSSMANN
Casting .... AMY LIEBERMAN
Production Stage Manager................ BOBBY DELUCA
Stage Manager .... VANESSA J. NOON
Coordinating Producer................ DOLORES CHAVEZ
Artistic Supervisor .... COREY MADDEN
Master Electrician .... EFRAIN MORALES
Production Assistant .... ROBERT BOYD
Crew Head/Audio Engineer............ JAMES WITHERALL
Tour Coordinator .... KIMIKO L. BRODER

THE HIGHEST HEAVEN

A Full-length Play
For 3 Men and 2 Women, some doubling

CHARACTERS

HURACAN . . . . a 12-year-old Latino boy.

EL NEGRO . . a Black man in his 50s. Worn like the earth,
he is troubled by his past.
Caretaker of the monarch butterflies.

KIKA . . . . Huracán's mother. A memory.
(May also play the WIFE)

DONA ELENA . . . . a dark-skinned Mexican widow.
Old, possessive, petty and disturbed.

MOISES, THE POLICE OFFICIAL, THE ADDICT, THE
UNDERTAKER-BARBER and the HUSBAND may be
played by one actor. A fool. Related to Doña Elena.

BUTTERFLY EFFECT: Both productions incorporated a small fan which was rigged below the stage. A small hole was cut on the stage floor to allow the actor to remove the cut piece and release the butterfly confetti over the fan allowing the butterflies to float high into the air. The floating butterflies seen throughout the play were rigged on long poles and manipulated by actors.

MUSIC: The Negro spirituals used in the play are believed to be public domain. They are: O, Sit Down Servant, Somebody's Calling My Name, Couldn't Hear Nobody Pray, Roll, Jordan, Roll. Music is available at the back of the playbook.

THE HIGHEST HEAVEN

SCENE 1

SETTING: *The 1930s when America was in the middle of the Depression. During that period thousands of Mexican nationals, as well as Americans of Mexican descent were repatriated to Mexico with or without their consent. The setting takes place in various locales and should only be suggestive. Title projections are optional. SOUND: A Negro spiritual is heard. Several monarch butterflies appear fluttering over the stage. Their wings glow, revealing deep vibrant colors.*

AT RISE: *"The Great Depression. October 1931. The monarch butterfly begins his journey.*—La gran Depresión. Octubre 1931. La mariposa monarca comienza su viaje venturoso." *SOUND: A train station. It is chaotic. Noisy. Dusty. Lights rise on a young Latino boy named HURACAN holding a suitcase. He is scared and alone. KIKA, Huracan's mother appears.*

KIKA. *Huracán!*
HURACAN. What is it, *'Amá?*
KIKA. Grab your things.
HURACAN. But why?
KIKA. They're taking us away.
HURACAN. Who is?

KIKA. Men with guns and badges!

HURACAN. Where are we going?

KIKA. They're taking us away on a train to Mexico!

HURACAN. But why?

KIKA. I don't know! Where's your father?

HURACAN. *'Apá* was right behind us.

KIKA. I've got to find him. Stay here.

HURACAN. Can't I go with you?

KIKA. I'll be right back. Everything is going to be fine.

HURACAN. How do you know?

KIKA. I just do.

(SOUND: Another train whistle blast is heard. HURA-CAN sits on a suitcase.)

KIKA. Remember, when you're scared God's watching.

(KIKA exits. EL NEGRO, an old black man, appears.)

EL NEGRO *(to HURACAN)*. Boy?

HURACAN. Huh?

EL NEGRO. That suitcase belongs to me.

HURACAN. My *'amá* told me to wait here.

EL NEGRO. You're sittin' on it.

HURACAN. That's what she said.

EL NEGRO. What are you lookin' at?

HURACAN. You must be *San Martin de Porres*.

EL NEGRO. Who?

HURACAN. The patron saint of the defenseless. Have you come to answer my prayer?

EL NEGRO. I ain't *San Martin*.

HURACAN. But he's black like you. Am I in heaven?

EL NEGRO. You ain't dead and I ain't no saint! This is *Misas*, Mexico, boy. Don't you know where you at?

HURACAN. No, my *'amá* said to stay here.

EL NEGRO. They all gone, boy. You're on your own. *Andale*, I got a train to catch. *(HURACAN watches as EL NEGRO picks up his suitcase and waits for the train. Then ...)* I can't do it. I can't get on. *(EL NEGRO exits as the train leaves.)*

HURACAN *(yelling)*. *'Amá!*

SCENE 2

"Far from home a small caterpillar searches for food.— Lejos de su casa una pequeña oruga busca comida." No- vember. *El dia de los muertos—The Day of the Dead. A cemetery. A remembrance for the dead. Like a Diego Rivera painting shawled women kneel whispering prayers before the graves of their dead. Candles burn, fresh cempasúchil (marigolds) flowers adorn, candy skulls and bread lie out on plates inviting the lost souls to partake. A wealthy woman, DONA ELENA, dressed in black, and her servant, MOISES, enter. DONA ELENA stands before her husband's tomb.*

DONA ELENA. Help me down, *Moises.*

MOISES. *Sí, Doña Elena.*

DONA ELENA. Bring me his basket.

MOISES. Here it is, *Doña Elena.*

DONA ELENA *(kneels at a grave)*. *Porfirio*, my dear sweet dead husband, I bring you wine from your vineyard, bread from your bakery and meat from your *rancho*. *(To MOISES.)* What are you looking at, *Indio?*

MOISES. Nothing, *Doña Elena.*

DONA ELENA. Turn your back and cover your ears. This conversation doesn't concern you.

MOISES. *Sí, Doña Elena. (He turns his back and covers his ears.)*

DONA ELENA. I'm afraid I don't trust your unwanted son, *Porfirio.* You created him but he's nothing like you. None of those "cousins" are. There's the banker, the bread maker, the harlot, the nun, the police official, the addict and this *Indio* half-breed. Your infidelities have cost me dearly, *Querido.* I spit on you. *(She spits and then crosses herself.)* But I remember you, husband, as a faithful wife should on the Day of the Dead. I want all of those "cousins" to know how loyal I am. *(Pause.)* It gets me things.

(HURACAN enters and crosses to DONA ELENA.)

HURACAN. *Señora*, may I have a piece of sweetbread?

DONA ELENA. No, you may not. This food belongs to me and my dead husband.

HURACAN. But I'm hungry.

DONA ELENA. Begging won't do you any good. I gave at church. *Moises?!*

HURACAN. Please, I haven't eaten all day.

DONA ELENA. I don't care! *Moises?! (She hits MOISES with her cane. He uncovers his ears.)*

MOISES. *Ay! Doña Elena?*

DONA ELENA. What are you doing?

MOISES. Talking to the spirits, *Doña.*

DONA ELENA. Crazy *Indio*. Help me up. Go away, you wretched boy.

MOISES. You heard the *Señora*. Go!

HURACAN. But I'm dizzy from hunger.

DONA ELENA *(tempting him)*. Then take the bread.

MOISES. *Doña?*

DONA ELENA. Be my guest.

HURACAN. Thank you, *Señora. (HURACAN reaches for the sweetbread and DONA ELENA hits him with her cane.)* Ouch!

DONA ELENA. Stupid boy. I said, "no" the first time. Now do you understand? My possessions are not to be touched. Not! Not! Not! *(HURACAN hides.) Moises*, you should be more attentive.

MOISES. *Sí, Doña Elena.*

DONA ELENA. I tire of this country's filth, its lack of culture and mostly of its poor. My dead husband and I started with nothing. We became quite successful and respected. Why must we carry the poor on our backs?

MOISES. I don't know ...

(DONA ELENA hits MOISES with her cane.)

DONA ELENA. I wasn't speaking to you. If only you had lived, *Querido*. We would have been rid of *El Negro* by now. Taken what's ours. Everyone would fear us. But you died too soon. Once again, leaving me to clean up your mess. *El Negro* is like a cancer. How I hate him. But I'll find a way. Find his weakness. Then strike. *(To MOISES.)* Why hasn't *Don Porfirio's* tomb been cleaned? I'm ashamed at how dirty it looks. There's dust everywhere. One can never be clean in this godforsaken country. Take me home!

(DONA ELENA and MOISES exit, HURACAN begins to eat as incense burns and prayers are whispered. MOISES reenters.)

MOISES. The dead must be respected, *muchacho.* Leave an offering.
HURACAN. Huh?

(MOISES places some coins on the tombstone.)

MOISES. If *Doña Elena* catches you we'll both be in trouble. Serious trouble. *(MOISES begins collecting food from other tombs and placing it on Don Porfirio's tomb.)* She's going to tell my cousin, the police official, and he'll come looking for you. You better leave now. You can't stay here. She does hateful things to people, especially children.
HURACAN. Have you seen my *'amá?* I lost her at the train station.
MOISES. No, I'm sorry, I haven't. But what do you expect? The whole station was a disaster. It's been like that all month. People everywhere. Screaming and crying. It makes no sense. And now everyone's gone.
HURACAN. Do you know where the train went?
MOISES. Maybe south. I'm not sure.
HURACAN. But I have to find my *'amá.*
MOISES. You can't go back there. Not even into town. *Doña Elena* has spies everywhere.
HURACAN. Please help me.

MOISES. There's nothing I can do. If *Doña Elena* knew I was talking to you...

HURACAN. I want my *'amá*.

(SOUND: A coyote's howl is heard off in the distance.)

MOISES. Perhaps you can go into the forest.

HURACAN. Forest?

MOISES. That's where *El Negro* lives. Nobody ever goes there. Everyone's afraid of him, but not me. I'll go find him for you. But if *Doña Elena* finds out I helped you...

HURACAN. I won't say a word.

MOISES. Good. Here, take this blanket. It'll be cold tonight. It's all I can give you. And remember my cousin will be looking for you.

HURACAN. Who?

MOISES. The police official.

(MOISES exits. HURACAN wraps himself in the blanket. A moment later he pushes everything off the tomb in anger.)

HURACAN. Why is this happening to me?! Where are you, *'Amá?*

("The small caterpillar remembers his past.—La oruga pequeña recuerda su pasado." El valle—*The valley appears. A barn sits on the edge of a green field and the valley is filled with blue sky. KIKA, Huracán's mother, enters carrying a laundry basket.)*

KIKA. *Huracán*, you've got chores!

HURACAN. But I'm hungry, *'Amá.*

KIKA. There's plenty of time to eat later.

HURACAN. I hate chores, *'Amá.* Why can't we have a maid like in the movies?

KIKA. *Andale!*

(She takes the bread away and hands HURACAN a coffee can. He begins to feed the imaginary chickens.)

HURACAN. It's so hopeless. Things only get messy again.

KIKA. If everyone went around thinking like that nothing would ever get done. Laundry would never get washed. Rooms would never get cleaned. Your socks and *chonies* would never get starched and ironed.

HURACAN. It would be my kind of heaven.

KIKA. Well, heaven wouldn't be very clean now, would it? God would be very unhappy. Angels flying with filthy wings? *Imposible.*

(SOUND: A train whistle is heard off in the distance.)

HURACAN. The train's on time!

KIKA. I hate how it rumbles past our home. There's dust everywhere. My heaven is going to be a place without railroads and trains or specks of dirt anywhere. Your father promised he'd be back now. We live in the United States where everything's on time except for him. *(A little worried.)* Where can he be?

HURACAN. Maybe he's buying something.

KIKA. He won't go into town. It isn't safe. People are being sent away. So, you stay near me.

HURACAN. Do you know what's today, *'Amá?*

KIKA. It's Tuesday.

HURACAN. Yeah, but it's not just any Tuesday. There's something special about this Tuesday. Remember?

KIKA. No.

HURACAN. *'Amá.*

KIKA. Of course I remember! You're growing so quickly. You'll never be eleven again. *(She kisses him on the cheek.)*

HURACAN. So?

KIKA. So?

HURACAN. So, is there anything I should open now, *'Amá?*

KIKA. Ay, *Huracán*, can't you wait to celebrate tonight?

HURACAN. No!

KIKA. You're just like your father. *Imposible. (She gives HURACAN a small gift wrapped in burlap.)* Happy Birthday, *Huracán!*

(HURACAN immediately opens it. It is a glass jar with a monarch butterfly.)

HURACAN. It's a butterfly!

KIKA. It's not just any butterfly, *Huracán.* It's a *monarca.* A king butterfly.

HURACAN. What am I supposed to do with it?

KIKA. Make a wish and then let it go.

HURACAN. But I want to keep it.

KIKA. It isn't for you to keep.

HURACAN. But what kind of gift is that, if I can't keep it?

KIKA. You're suppose to make a wish. Then let it go, and your wish will come true.

HURACAN. Will my butterfly ever come back?

KIKA. No, but one of his children might. And when he
    returns, *Huracán*, there'll be thousands of monarchs with
    him dancing like leaves in the wind. They'll stop here to
    rest their weary wings and quench their thirsty mouths.
    When they do we'll dampen the earth with fresh water.

HURACAN. Why?

KIKA. So the flowers will be strong to feed these *maripo-
    sas* their sweet nectar. It's a glimpse at God's heart.

HURACAN. God's heart?

KIKA. It's a blessing, *mijo*.

HURACAN. How come you know so much about things?

KIKA. Not everything comes out of a book, *Huracán*. Who
    taught you to tell time by reading the sun?

HURACAN. You did.

KIKA. Who taught you to eat cactus without pricking your-
    self?

HURACAN. You.

KIKA. There are many ways to learn and they don't all
    come from a book. The earth has secrets. If you watch
    and listen closely she'll share them with you.

HURACAN *(closing his eyes)*. Okay. Done. Time to go,
    mariposa. Fly!

*(HURACAN opens the jar and releases the butterfly. The
monarch butterfly flutters off into the blue sky. SOUND:
A siren is heard. KIKA sees something off in the distance.)*

HURACAN. What is it, *'Amá?*

KIKA. Oh, no, they're coming this way!

HURACAN. Who is?

KIKA. Men with guns and badges!

HURACAN. Why?

KIKA. There's no time to explain. We have to go!

HURACAN. But my butterfly king. I've got to save him!

KIKA. No, *Huracán*, there isn't time!

HURACAN. He won't make it by himself!

KIKA. *Huracán!*

(A dust storm arrives. A moment later HURACAN struggles to awaken from his nightmare. DONA ELENA enters standing over him.)

DONA ELENA. Wake up! Wake up, you!

HURACAN. *'Amá?*

DONA ELENA. How dare you call me your mother! I'm nobody's mother! You little thief, you've taken food from my dead husband! *(She begins beating him with her cane.)*

HURACAN. No! Stop hitting me!

DONA ELENA. I'll teach you never to steal from the dead! *Toma!*

(EL NEGRO enters and crosses to DONA ELENA taking away her cane.)

EL NEGRO. Leave the boy alone!

DONA ELENA. How dare you interfere, *Negro!*

EL NEGRO. What's he done?

DONA ELENA. He's a thief!

HURACAN. I was hungry.

DONA ELENA *(grabs HURACAN by the ear)*. Do you know what I do to horrible little children?

HURACAN. Ouch!

EL NEGRO. Leave the boy alone!

DONA ELENA. Give me back my cane, *Negro! (EL NE-GRO holds the cane up as if to strike her. She releases HURACAN.)* How dare you try to strike me!

EL NEGRO. I ain't yet, but I might. Get up, boy.

DONA ELENA. I promise you'll pay for this insult!

EL NEGRO. Get in line.

DONA ELENA. Crazy old *gringo*, Protector of the butterflies and now children too? Saint *El Negro*, is it?

EL NEGRO. This ain't got nothin' to do with saints.

DONA ELENA. That's right, *Negro*. How can I forget? There's unfinished business between you and me.

EL NEGRO. The boy's got nothin' to do with it.

DONA ELENA. I'll see you dead yet.

EL NEGRO. Them mountain spirits got powerful magic.

DONA ELENA. How frightening. But it's a matter of time. I have it and you don't.

EL NEGRO. You ain't won yet.

DONA ELENA. When I do I'll dance on your grave.

EL NEGRO. I ain't afraid of you. Everybody knows it. People laughin' at you 'cause you ain't got rid of me yet.

DONA ELENA *(to EL NEGRO)*. Just wait! *(EL NEGRO lets out a loud howl. To HURACAN:)* Your selfishness will cost you too, boy, mark my words! *Ay! Oficial?! Oficial?! (She exits.)*

EL NEGRO. You better go. She'll be back soon.

HURACAN. Which way did my *'amá's* train go?

EL NEGRO. That old spider has no compassion in her.

HURACAN. Will it come back?

EL NEGRO. *Andale!* Go!

(EL NEGRO exits quickly. HURACAN grabs as much bread as he can as the POLICE OFFICIAL races in. He is the same actor who plays MOISES. The POLICE OFFICIAL wears a mustache, a uniform and holds a revolver in one hand and a lantern in the other.)

POLICE OFFICIAL *(frightened). Negro? (No answer.)* Oh, thank God. *(HURACAN tries to exit.)* Who's there?

HURACAN *(freezing).* ...

POLICE OFFICIAL. Is that you, beggar boy? What have you done to *Doña Elena?* She's erupted like a volcano spewing curses at everyone. No one will sleep tonight. Beggar boy?

HURACAN. ...

(HURACAN covers himself with the blanket. The POLICE OFFICIAL shines the light toward HURACAN.)

POLICE OFFICIAL. Oh, forgive me, *Señora?* Or is *Señor?*

HURACAN. ...

POLICE OFFICIAL. *Ah, Señor!*

(HURACAN nods his head "Yes." From beneath HURACAN's blanket a piece of sweetbread falls to the ground. The POLICE OFFICIAL picks it up.)

POLICE OFFICIAL *(suddenly).* What are you doing with *Don Porfirio's* sweetbread?! *(HURACAN accidentally drops more bread onto the ground.) Ay!* It can't be? Can it? *Don Porfirio?* Is that you?

HURACAN *(dropping his voice). Sí.*

POLICE OFFICIAL. *Sí!* Of course it's you! It's the Day of the Dead. Are you well, Father?

HURACAN *(dropping his voice)*. No.

POLICE OFFICIAL *(to himself)*. No! You fool, how can he be well? He's dead! *(To HURACAN.)* I'm not use to talking to the dead, Father. Um, did you happen to see a beggar boy come this way?

HURACAN *(dropping his voice)*. No. *(HURACAN begins to walk away as the bread he collected keeps falling to the ground.)*

POLICE OFFICIAL. Wait! *(HURACAN freezes.)* You dropped this, Father. *(He hands HURACAN all the sweetbread.)*

HURACAN. *Gracias.*

POLICE OFFICIAL. *No hay de que.* Forgive me for disturbing your meal, Father. I mean no harm.

HURACAN. Boo!

POLICE OFFICIAL. *Ay!*

(The POLICE OFFICIAL exits out quickly. HURACAN exits the other way.)

SCENE 3

"Butterfly sanctuary. Deep within the forest. The caterpillar finds a home.—Santuario de las mariposas. Un bosque, la oruga encuentra un hogar.*" EL NEGRO sits by a fire. He opens his suitcase. It glows from within. He senses something wrong. EL NEGRO closes his suitcase and picks up a large stick.*

EL NEGRO *(calling out).* Who's out there?

HURACAN. ...

EL NEGRO. *Doña Elena?*

HURACAN. No.

EL NEGRO. Is that you, boy?

HURACAN. Yes.

EL NEGRO. How long you been there watchin'?

HURACAN. Forever.

EL NEGRO. What's your business?

HURACAN. I'm hungry. May I have something to eat?

EL NEGRO. I don't take freeloaders. What's you got to trade?

HURACAN. I can work for my food.

EL NEGRO *(laughing).* You mean you gonna pull your own weight like a man? With them skinny arms?

HURACAN. What's wrong with my arms?

EL NEGRO. They skinny! *(EL NEGRO coughs.)*

HURACAN. Stop laughing at me! I don't need your help, old man! I can do this all by myself!

EL NEGRO. Then go! No one stoppin' you!

HURACAN. Okay, I'm goin'! *(HURACAN stops.)*

EL NEGRO. Well, I'm waitin'!

HURACAN. I'm real hungry!

EL NEGRO *(throws HURACAN some food).* Eat, boy. Then go! *(Singing.)*

O, sit down, servant, sit down;

O, sit down, servant...

HURACAN. Why did that old woman beat me?

EL NEGRO. You probably had it comin'.

HURACAN. I didn't do nothing to her.

EL NEGRO. 'Cept steal her food.

HURACAN. I was hungry.

EL NEGRO. She's a nasty old crow. Dangerous too. Her name is *Doña Elena*. Wealthiest woman in town. Owns everything 'cept these woods and she wants them too.

HURACAN. Why?

EL NEGRO. 'Cause she gotta possess everythin' there is. Take my soul if she could. Cut them trees down and sell it as lumber.

HURACAN. She called you a crazy *gringo*. Are you?

EL NEGRO. I can howl at the moon and make it disappear.

HURACAN. No, you can't. *(EL NEGRO howls. And the moon disappears.)* How'd you do that?

EL NEGRO. That's a secret.

HURACAN. It's a stupid trick.

EL NEGRO. Ain't no trick. That's coyote talk. Where you from, boy?

HURACAN. ... *(HURACAN crosses his arms.)*

EL NEGRO. Oh, so now you ain't talkin'?

HURACAN. ...

EL NEGRO. I bet you must be from California.

HURACAN. How do you know that?

EL NEGRO. 'Cause that attitude of yours is as big as that state. Gots to be California.

HURACAN. So what if I am?

EL NEGRO. That means you and me from Gringoland. You a long ways from home.

HURACAN. Me and my *'amá* got sent here.

(SOUND: A train is heard rolling through the night. A boxcar interior appears. KIKA enters. HURACAN joins her.)

KIKA. *Huracán!*

HURACAN. I'm right here, *'Amá*.

KIKA. Stay where I can see you.

HURACAN. Okay. Where's *'Apá?*

KIKA. He must be on another boxcar. *(She begins to cry softly.)*

HURACAN. Are you crying, *'Amá?*

KIKA. No, my eyes are just tired. Go to sleep. *(Pause.)*

HURACAN. Have you ever been on a train before, *'Amá?*

KIKA. No.

HURACAN. It's one of the most best things you can do. I mean, look out there?

KIKA. There's nothing to see.

HURACAN. The moon's out, *'Amá*. The earth has secrets. If you watch and listen she'll share them with you, remember? Look at the white clouds glow. You can see the shapes of family faces. See? There's *Nana Licha*...

KIKA. You're right.

HURACAN. And *Tia Lupe*.

KIKA. And there's our *primo, Conejo*.

HURACAN & KIKA *(placing their fingers on their head and making rabbit ears)*. Rabbit cousin!

HURACAN. Riding a train isn't so bad, is it, *'Amá?*

KIKA. I guess not. Say a prayer to *San Martin*. *(Sadly.)* Happy twelfth birthday, *Huracán*.

(The boxcar fades away. HURACAN joins EL NEGRO.)

EL NEGRO. You got "Repatriated." *(He hands HURACAN some more food.)*

HURACAN. What's that mean?

EL NEGRO. It means *los norte gringos* don't want you in their stinking country. That's why they sent you away.

HURACAN. But why would they send me here? Mexico isn't my country.

EL NEGRO. They in a "Depression." Country's broke.

HURACAN. I broke nothing.

EL NEGRO. Depression's made people crazy. Plenty of trains been comin' through *Misas* lately. Lots of folk. Steppin' outta them boxcars. Carryin' what they own. Old men, women and children all lookin' like they come outta the Bible. Like them Israelites leavin' Egypt. Searchin' for the Promised Land. 'Cept this ain't Egypt and they ain't got Moses.

HURACAN. Will you help me find my *'amá?*

EL NEGRO. Ain't my business. You got to learn to help yourself. Understand? But you best wait 'til *Doña Elena* forgets about you 'fore you go into town. *(EL NEGRO prepares to sleep near the fire. Sings.)*

O, sit down, servant, sit down;
Sit down and rest a little while.

You snore?

HURACAN. No.

EL NEGRO. Good. You can sleep here tonight. But tomorrow you go. *(EL NEGRO lies down to sleep. So does HURACAN.)*

HURACAN. *Señor?*

EL NEGRO. What?

HURACAN. Do you have anything else to eat?

SCENE 4

"The caterpillar becomes a chrysalis changing form and color.—La oruga se transforma en una crisálida, cambiando de forma y color." At the train station. SOUND:

Voices from EL NEGRO's haunting past are heard. EL NEGRO stands holding his suitcase and a train ticket.

EL NEGRO. I can't do it. I can't get on. *(Pause.)* Yeah. Made them *Indios* a promise. Somebody's gotta look after them monarchs.

(He tears up the ticket. He coughs. The train departs. He exits as HURACAN rushes in picking up the torn pieces. He looks at it. SOUND: A train is heard. KIKA appears as a memory.)

KIKA. *Huracán! (She crosses to him.)*
HURACAN. *'Amá?*
KIKA. Hold this. *(She places a handful of earth onto HURACAN's palm.)*
HURACAN. What is it?
KIKA. Smell it!
HURACAN. Why?
KIKA. Do as I say!
HURACAN *(smells it)*. It's just dirt.
KIKA. It's more than that! Taste it!
HURACAN. No, *'Amá!*
KIKA. Do as I tell you!
HURACAN *(tastes the earth)*. Aagghh...
KIKA. This soil is from the valley you come from. You mustn't ever forget
HURACAN. I won't. *(He cleans his mouth.)*
KIKA. You've tasted it. It's in your body now. Our valley will always be your home. No matter what happens. Remember. Promise me.

HURACAN. Okay, I promise. *(KIKA begins to back away.)*
    Where are you going, *'Amá?*
KIKA. To look for your *'apá.* Stay here.
HURACAN. Can't I go with you?
KIKA. I'll be right back. Everything is going to be fine.
HURACAN. How do you know?
KIKA. I just do.

(Lights fade.)

SCENE 5

"Walking among the sleeping monarchs.—Caminando
entre las mariposas monarcas dormidas." *The sun whispers in the night. EL NEGRO holds a dead butterfly in
his palm.*

EL NEGRO. *Mariposa*, you've traveled such a long way
    only to die. Was it worth it? *(He buries the butterfly. He
    hears something off in the distance. He picks up his
    stick.)* Who's out there?
HURACAN. ...
EL NEGRO. Boy?
HURACAN. Yes.

(HURACAN enters.)

EL NEGRO. Why do you keep followin' me?
HURACAN. I don't like to be alone.
EL NEGRO. Come here. *(HURACAN comes closer.)* Closer.
    (HURACAN crosses cautiously towards EL NEGRO.) You

don't spy on people 'cause they're gonna think you're a snake. And you know what happens to snakes?

HURACAN. They get hit?

EL NEGRO. They ain't got friends. *(EL NEGRO puts the stick down.)*

HURACAN. Oh...

EL NEGRO. Sit down. *(HURACAN sits on EL NEGRO's suitcase.)* Not there! That's my baggage!

HURACAN. What's in it?

EL NEGRO. Ghosts! You wanna see?

HURACAN *(afraid)*. Uh-uh!!

EL NEGRO. Them cousins are afraid of it too. Got powerful magic. *Doña Elena* lookin' to take it from me. But she can't 'cause I won't let her. Nobody comes near it. Understand?

HURACAN. I won't touch it.

EL NEGRO. Good. I suppose you want somethin' to eat?

HURACAN. I'll work for it.

EL NEGRO. You gonna pull your own weight?

HURACAN. I will.

EL NEGRO. There ain't gonna be no complainin'.

HURACAN. Okay.

EL NEGRO. I like my peace. *(They sit and eat.)*

HURACAN. Why do you live here? *(EL NEGRO shoots him a look. Pause. He hands EL NEGRO some sweetbread.)*

EL NEGRO. Where'd you get this?

HURACAN. I stole it.

EL NEGRO. Ain't right for a boy to steal.

HURACAN. Ain't right I'm in Mexico! Ain't right I've been beaten! Ain't right my *'amá's* gone!

EL NEGRO. Now, hold on there. All I'm sayin' is, it ain't right. That's all. A man's gotta do what he's gotta do.

HURACAN. Well, I'm doin' it!

EL NEGRO. You in a nasty mood. Man's gotta have himself a sense of humor. Be able to laugh at his self. It helps cut the pain, boy. Understand? It's good bread. Hard, but good. *(HURACAN shrugs his shoulders.)* Look up in them trees.

HURACAN. What are they?

EL NEGRO. Them's monarchs.

HURACAN. Monarch butterflies? What are they doing up there?

EL NEGRO. It's where they live. This here is *Santuario de las Mariposas.*

HURACAN. Is this where they come to?

EL NEGRO. Every year.

HURACAN. I wonder which one is mine?

EL NEGRO. What?

HURACAN. Why are they bunched together like that in the trees?

EL NEGRO. Maybe to keep warm. Maybe for protection.

HURACAN. There must be millions of them.

EL NEGRO. Wait 'til the sun warms them. It's a beautiful sight when they dance in the air. The *Indios* believe that the souls of the dead are carried up to heaven on the backs of butterflies. You think it's true? *(HURACAN shrugs his shoulders.)* I want to believe. Believe in somethin'.

HURACAN. I want to be eleven again.

EL NEGRO. Pretty soon their children will come out of them cocoons, dry their wings in the warm sun and start flyin' home.

HURACAN. I want to be in my home and my 'amá waiting there for me. It's not fair! Why did this happen to me! I want everything back the way it was! I want to wake up in my bed...

EL NEGRO. Listen here, boy...

HURACAN. I hate Mexico!

EL NEGRO. There once was a butterfly who wanted to be a caterpillar. Yeah. You see, them seasons started changin' and lots of them monarchs got to dyin'. So the butterfly asked the great Creator to change him back to a caterpillar. The great Creator told him he was gonna give the butterfly a gift but he had to stay a butterfly. "You gonna carry the souls of the dead humans up to heaven. And your children and your children's children too." "But I want to be caterpillar again," said the monarch. "Let them other butterflies fly to heaven." Well, that butterfly got his wish and became a caterpillar once more. He was so happy he began dancin' 'cept he slipped off a leaf and landed right into a black spider's web. Bam! Never knew what hit him.

HURACAN. Why are you telling me this?

EL NEGRO. You can never go back. Our lives are measured by moments. And them moments change your life forever. Sometimes you gotta grow up sooner than you want. Gotta move on. Fact of life.

HURACAN. No! I don't want to be here!

EL NEGRO. This is all you got!

HURACAN. I don't want to be like you!

EL NEGRO. All you got is me!

HURACAN. No!

EL NEGRO. Your mama ain't comin' back!

HURACAN. I did what she told me! I waited for her!

EL NEGRO. Get it through your head!

HURACAN. Why didn't she come back for me?

EL NEGRO. Maybe she tried! Maybe the train never stopped! Maybe—

HURACAN. Why didn't she come back?

(HURACAN cries. EL NEGRO reaches out to comfort the boy but stops himself.)

EL NEGRO. You a *cabezon!* And lazy too!

HURACAN. What are you talking about?

EL NEGRO. Where's my wood? Said you was gonna get me some. Man's gotta keep his word.

HURACAN. I ain't a man!

EL NEGRO. Well, I'm treatin' you like one. *(Starts coughing.)* Get use to it.

HURACAN. That's blood.

EL NEGRO. Ain't nothin'! Now go get me my wood!

SCENE 6

"The Black Widow spider spins her web.—La Viuda Negra hila su telaraña." *DONA ELENA sits near her husband's tomb. She takes out a cigar.*

DONA ELENA. From the grave you do me no good, *Porfirio*. Between all those cousins they can't capture one small boy and a howling old man. Why are they all so afraid of him? Stupid superstitious nincompoops. Magic spells, prayers and potions are the poor's only answer to reality. I need someone with intelligence, discretion and resourcefulness. Someone desperate. Someone with needs. Someone with a bad habit.

(THE ADDICT appears. He lights DONA ELENA's cigar. He is the same actor who played the POLICE OFFICIAL.)

THE ADDICT. You sent for me, *Doña Elena*.

DONA ELENA. I have work for you.

THE ADDICT. How wonderful it is to see you.

DONA ELENA. Be quiet. I want you to do a job for me. It must be done quickly and quietly.

THE ADDICT. What is it you ask?

DONA ELENA. Find a way to get *El Negro* and that boy off the mountain.

THE ADDICT. This will be very difficult. The land belongs to the *Indios*. *El Negro* is their friend. Besides he beats everyone who goes up there with a big stick.

DONA ELENA. I don't care how you do it! Just find a way. I won't be made a fool of. I hate that black man.

THE ADDICT. But you're Black.

DONA ELENA. No, I'm not. I'm Spanish.

THE ADDICT. You're part Black.

DONA ELENA. I'm Spanish I tell you!

THE ADDICT. But you're ...

DONA ELENA. Shut up, *idiota! (She hits THE ADDICT with her cane.)* Now, find a way to get *El Negro* off my mountain! I want that land and that suitcase. They should belong to me.

THE ADDICT. What's in it?

DONA ELENA. It's not your concern. Something valuable only to me. Just bring it.

THE ADDICT. Revenge does have its price, *Doña*.

DONA ELENA. I see you have your father's knack for business and his addiction.

THE ADDICT. We all have our crosses to bear.

(DONA ELENA hands THE ADDICT money. They exit.)

SCENE 7

"Within the chrysalis a metamorphosis begins.—Dentro de la crisálida comienza una metamorfosis." *HURACAN and EL NEGRO sit by a campfire. HURACAN has grown out of his old clothes. He eats quickly.*

EL NEGRO. Slow down! You gonna get yourself sick!

HURACAN. But I'm hungry.

EL NEGRO. You're like them monarch caterpillars. They eat everythin' in sight. They called *orugas*. That's what you are. An *oruga!*

HURACAN. I ain't no *oruga!*

EL NEGRO. Well, you eat like one! You been growin' out of them clothes and eatin' everything in sight for the last few months. Pretty soon you gonna be growin' hair in places you never thought you could!

HURACAN. No, I'm not!

EL NEGRO. Voice is gonna drop. Face gonna get bumpy and you gonna have thoughts about them females.

HURACAN. Is that wrong?

EL NEGRO. Ain't nothin' wrong with it. It's nature's way of makin' you a man. Like them *orugas* becomin' monarchs.

HURACAN. I'm startin' to forget things.

EL NEGRO. What things?

HURACAN. My *'amá's* voice. My *amá's* face.

EL NEGRO. Come spring them monarchs gonna leave. Under them milkweed plants they're growin' big. Changin' form. Preparin' themselves for the trip home. You think it's true them monarchs carry the souls of them dead humans to heaven?

HURACAN. I don't know. *(Two butterflies fall to the ground fighting.)* Why do the monarchs fight like that?

EL NEGRO. You ever been in love?

HURACAN. I love my mother.

EL NEGRO. That's not the same kind of love. See that male monarch is courtin' the female. They catch each other in the air and fall to the ground. Now, he'll try to woo her. And if she wants him she'll close her wings and he'll carry her to the tops of them trees and... *(The monarchs fly away. EL NEGRO begins laughing.)*

HURACAN *(disgusted)*. Ugghhh...

EL NEGRO. One day you gonna be just like this male. And hairy too!

HURACAN *(embarrassed)*. Ugghhh...

EL NEGRO. Fact of life.

HURACAN. I wanna go home. Look for my *'amá* and *'apá.*

EL NEGRO. When I first come here, this was the only place I could stay. Now, it's the only place I wanna stay. This here is sacred land. Nature's church.

HURACAN. Don't you got any family?

EL NEGRO. Them monarchs are my family now.

HURACAN. There's no one?

EL NEGRO. No.

(SOUND: A train whistle is heard off in the distance.)

HURACAN. How come you always got that suitcase with you?

EL NEGRO. I told you. Me and that suitcase ain't your business.

HURACAN. You walk to the station. I see you.

EL NEGRO. Why you gotta do that?

HURACAN. Do what?

EL NEGRO. Get in my business?

HURACAN. 'Cause you wanna leave without me.

EL NEGRO. I'm still here, ain't I?

HURACAN. I see you standin' there, but you don't get on the train. What's stoppin' you?

EL NEGRO. Listen here, every man has got to have a code to guide him through life. A system of rules to live by. I call them my "Don'ts." "Don't let anybody know your business. Don't walk away from a fight. Don't borrow money if you can't pay it back and don't mess with people 'cause they might mess you up." These been my guiding principles through life. You best learn it!

HURACAN. Then how do I get home?

EL NEGRO. Home?

HURACAN. What'da I gotta do?

EL NEGRO. You got a train ticket?

HURACAN. No!

EL NEGRO. You got any money?

HURACAN. No!

EL NEGRO. Then you outta luck! *(EL NEGRO coughs.)*

HURACAN. You coughing up blood again.

EL NEGRO. 'Cause it's a curse.

HURACAN. Was it *Doña Elena?*

EL NEGRO. It was long before her. Another lifetime. Things I wish I could change but can't. *(Singing.)*
Hush, hush,
Somebody's calling my name,
Hush, hush,
Somebody's calling my name,
HURACAN. Did you do something bad?
EL NEGRO. Ain't no one gonna forgive what I done.
HURACAN. You can't go back, can you?
EL NEGRO *(singing)*.
O, my Lord,
O, my Lord,
What shall I do?
HURACAN. Guardin' them monarchs is your penance, ain't it?

SCENE 8

"The dreams of butterflies.—Los sueños de las maripo-sas." *Dawn. SOUND: Voices from EL NEGRO's past are heard once again. HURACAN and EL NEGRO sleep by a smoldering fire. THE ADDICT sneaks in quietly. He opens his knife.*

EL NEGRO *(in his sleep)*. Snake eye starin' at me. Don't! Ain't gettin' onboard. No! Ain't afraid of no man. Beast. Night. Snake eye. No!

(THE ADDICT picks up EL NEGRO's suitcase and opens it with his knife. The suitcase glows. He smiles. HURACAN awakens seeing THE ADDICT.)

EL NEGRO *(in his sleep).* Ain't my time. No! Stay away.

THE ADDICT *(startled, mocking EL NEGRO).* El Diablo, huh! *(He crosses to finish EL NEGRO off. HURACAN howls, throwing his blanket over THE ADDICT. Frightened:)* El Diablo! *(THE ADDICT drops the suitcase and runs off.)*

HURACAN. Wake up, old man!

EL NEGRO. What is it?

HURACAN. Are you all right?

EL NEGRO. What's goin' on?

HURACAN. Somebody tried takin' your suitcase, but I scared him away. Just like you show me. *(HURACAN howls.)*

EL NEGRO. Was it one of them cousins?

HURACAN. I think so.

EL NEGRO. That old crow is gettin' desperate. Ain't no tellin' what she'll do. You better be careful.

HURACAN. They can't catch me. I'm too fast. I'm a coyote! *(HURACAN howls. EL NEGRO starts to cough.)* You're coughin' up more blood.

EL NEGRO. I got consumption. Tuberculosis.

HURACAN. Is it bad?

EL NEGRO. Ain't good.

HURACAN. Are you gonna die?

EL NEGRO. Hell no!

HURACAN. I'm just askin'.

EL NEGRO. I ain't dead yet. So don't you try buryin' me 'fore my time. I gots too much fight in me yet. *(He coughs again.)* Bring that blanket here! And put some more wood on that fire!

HURACAN. Okay! *(He picks up the blanket, and throws it at EL NEGRO.)*

SCENE 9

*"The spider captures her prey.—*La araña atrapa a su victima.*" The police station walls are filled with massive cracks as if a great weight rests on them. HURACAN's hands are tied and he is dragged in by the POLICE OF-FICIAL. The POLICE OFFICIAL is the same actor who plays THE ADDICT. He is eating some chocolate candy.*

POLICE OFFICIAL. Come here, boy! You're one of those *deportados*, aren't you? Thousands have been coming through town. It hasn't been this busy since *Pancho Villa* and the entire revolution rode through!

(DONA ELENA enters.)

POLICE OFFICIAL. *Doña Elena*, good morning. I found the beggar boy! I found him wandering around looking at girls.

DONA ELENA. Shut up! You dishonor your father. Look at you. Stay out of the sun. And lose some weight.

POLICE OFFICIAL. *Sí, Doña.*

DONA ELENA. Beggar boy, stealing from the dead and assaulting me on a holy day has its consequences.

HURACAN. That was a long time ago.

DONA ELENA. Eleven months. Twelve days. Six hours. Thirty-one seconds. I've burned you into my memory. One of my husband's sons is the town judge. He'll throw you in jail. I could see to it!

HURACAN. I don't want to go to jail.

POLICE OFFICIAL. But you're already in jail!

DONA ELENA. Shut up! Turn around and cover your ears! This conversation doesn't concern you!

POLICE OFFICIAL. *Sí, Doña Elena. (The POLICE OFFICIAL turns around and covers his ears.)* Tell me, why does *El Negro* hate me?

HURACAN. ...

DONA ELENA. We used to be friends.

HURACAN. ...

DONA ELENA. You know, when *El Negro* came to *Misas* we offered him a job. He took our money and betrayed us. My poor husband went to his grave because he was so heartbroken. He left me all alone just like you.

HURACAN. May I go now?

DONA ELENA. You poor boy. By yourself without a mother. How terrifying it must be.

HURACAN. I can take care of myself.

DONA ELENA. Of course you can. If you were my child I would never have left you. I couldn't live with myself.

HURACAN. Well, maybe my *'amá* tried.

DONA ELENA. Maybe...

HURACAN. And maybe she's still looking for me.

DONA ELENA. Maybe, but if she really loved you, don't you think she would have found you by now?

HURACAN. ...

DONA ELENA. But look how you've survived? You've triumphed over adversity. I admire that quality. It's sadly lacking in this town. You and I are very similar. We'll fight to survive.

HURACAN. It's not easy.

DONA ELENA. No one can appreciate the sacrifice but us. *(She caresses his face.)* Would you like a piece of candy?

HURACAN. Okay.

DONA ELENA. *Oficial! (The POLICE OFFICIAL doesn't hear her.) Oficial!! (He still doesn't hear her.) Oficial!!!*

(DONA ELENA strikes the POLICE OFFICIAL. He uncovers his ears and turns around.)

POLICE OFFICIAL. Ouch!! *Sí, Doña Elena?*
DONA ELENA. Why do these *tontos* all torment me?
POLICE OFFICIAL. I'm sorry, *Doña.*
DONA ELENA. Be quiet and give me a piece of *chocolate.*
POLICE OFFICIAL. But it's my last piece.
DONA ELENA. Give it to me! *(She reaches out and takes the candy from the POLICE OFFICIAL. To HURACAN:) Ay, Pobrecito. (HURACAN begins eating the chocolate candy.)* Is it good?
HURACAN. Ah huh.
DONA ELENA. Tell me, does *El Negro* ever talk about leaving?
HURACAN. Sometimes. I tell him he should go back home with me, but then he talks about his ghosts.
POLICE OFFICIAL. Ghosts? What ghosts?
HURACAN. They're in his suitcase. I'm not supposed to touch it.
DONA ELENA. His ghosts are a great burden. His soul riddled with pain. You see, he has a very dark secret.
HURACAN. What secret?
DONA ELENA. Hasn't he told you?
HURACAN. No.
DONA ELENA. It's in his suitcase. He's never without it. Tell me, do you miss your home?
HURACAN. Yes.

DONA ELENA. Your *'amá* could be there waiting for you, do you think? I bet she would be so happy to see you. I could help you, you know?

HURACAN. Help me?

DONA ELENA. Look what I've got for you. *(She holds up a train pass.)*

HURACAN. What is it?

DONA ELENA. A train ticket.

HURACAN. For me?

DONA ELENA. Yes. Just think, you could be with your *'amá. El Negro* at peace with himself.

POLICE OFFICIAL. And you'll have the suitcase!

DONA ELENA. Shut up, *idiota! (The POLICE OFFICIAL covers his ears. To HURACAN:)* All you have to do is bring *El Negro's* suitcase to me. Just pick it up and walk away. It's so simple. What do you say?

(HURACAN holds out his bound hands. DONA ELENA hits the POLICE OFFICIAL.)

POLICE OFFICIAL. Ouch!

DONA ELENA. Untie him. *(The POLICE OFFICIAL unties HURACAN's hands.)* Would you like another piece of candy? *(She smiles.)*

SCENE 10

"The monarch chooses.—La monarca hace su decision.*"* Santuario de las mariposas. *SOUND: A coyote's howl is heard off in the distance. HURACAN enters. The forest casts dark shadows.*

HURACAN. Old man? *(Pause.)* Are you here?

(HURACAN picks up the suitcase. SOUND: A distant train is heard. EL NEGRO enters wrapped in a blanket and carrying some wood. He appears frail. HURACAN doesn't see him. EL NEGRO watches as HURACAN stands there deciding what to do. HURACAN places the suitcase back.)

HURACAN. I can't do it. I can't.

EL NEGRO. She put you up to it?

HURACAN. ...

EL NEGRO. Why didn't you take it?

HURACAN. What's in it?

EL NEGRO. My life. *Doña Elena* thinks I still got her money, but I don't. I give it away to them *Indios* long ago, 'cause they was starvin'. I ruined her plans. Now, you too. She ain't gonna be too happy 'bout this.

HURACAN. I won't go back into town.

EL NEGRO. Won't matter. She'll find you.

HURACAN. I ain't afraid of her.

EL NEGRO. But you should be. There's no tellin' what she's gonna do now. It's time for you to go.

HURACAN. Go where?

EL NEGRO. Anyplace, but here.

HURACAN. I can't leave you.

EL NEGRO. Don't you see? It ain't safe. I can't protect you no more.

HURACAN. Then come back with me!

EL NEGRO. I can't.

HURACAN. Why not?

EL NEGRO. I can't go back.

HURACAN. I ain't leavin' you.

EL NEGRO. Pack your things and go!

HURACAN. We's friends!

EL NEGRO. I ain't your friend! Don't wanna be your friend! Ain't never had a friend. You just in the way.

HURACAN. No, I'm not!

EL NEGRO. And I'm through carrying you! So go!

HURACAN *(crying)*. But we's friends!

EL NEGRO. Get outta here! Get!

(HURACAN exits.)

SCENE 11

"The spider attacks.—La araña ataca." DONA ELENA and the UNDERTAKER-BARBER enter. The UNDER-TAKER-BARBER is played by the same actor who plays the POLICE OFFICIAL. He carries a shovel. They surprise EL NEGRO.

DONA ELENA. *Viejo Negro!*

EL NEGRO. So the black widow spider's finally come?

DONA ELENA. Is that how you treat an old friend, *Negro?*

EL NEGRO. What do you want?

DONA ELENA. Perhaps the Undertaker-Barber could help you understand what I want? I finally found someone who isn't afraid of you. He even brought his own shovel!

UNDERTAKER-BARBER Agghhh!

(The UNDERTAKER-BARBER lunges at EL NEGRO holding the shovel to his throat. HURACAN runs in.)

HURACAN. Let him go!

DONA ELENA. You don't give orders here. I do! *(She hits HURACAN with her cane.)*

HURACAN. Ouch!

DONA ELENA. We had a deal, *Cucaracha*, and you betrayed me. You should've left while you had the chance. Now you'll never see your mother. *(She tears up the train ticket.)* She'll wander the earth like *La Llorona* crying and tearing out her hair! *"Mijo! Mijo!"* *(To EL NEGRO.)* And you, *Negro*, we offered you a job, respect, wealth and you refused!

EL NEGRO. You wanted me to burn this forest!

HURACAN. He wouldn't do that!

DONA ELENA. He's done far worse!

EL NEGRO *(to DONA ELENA)*. I ain't that man no more!

DONA ELENA. Tell him, *Negro!* Tell him the truth why you can't go back to your own country. No matter how many times you've tried getting on board a train, you can't. Tell him why you're so afraid.

HURACAN. He ain't afraid of nothin'!

DONA ELENA. Then let me enlighten you, *Cucaracha*. Your patron saint of butterflies is a wanted man. A dead man. His ghosts are there waiting him.

EL NEGRO. Don't you say nothin'!

DONA ELENA. He won't tell you his terrible dark secret.

HURACAN. It don't matter!

DONA ELENA. But it does. He set a house on fire in your country.

EL NEGRO. Don't you believe her!

DONA ELENA *(mocking him)*. He had been wronged. Mistreated. His pride demanded revenge so he burned it to the ground. But in that house children were sleeping.

HURACAN. Children?

EL NEGRO. She ain't tellin' you everythin'!

DONA ELENA. Five little angels tucked away in their beds.

EL NEGRO. I was after the man who done me wrong!

DONA ELENA. He drenched the whole house with gasoline.

EL NEGRO. He stole my land. Burned my crops!

DONA ELENA. Lit a match and the whole house went up in flames. They couldn't get out. Only their cries got out. Calling for their mommy.

HURACAN. Is it true?

DONA ELENA. Tell him!

EL NEGRO. They wasn't supposed to be there!

HURACAN. How could you do that?

EL NEGRO. They wasn't supposed to be there!

DONA ELENA. Those little angels went to heaven and *El Diablo* ran away.

EL NEGRO. I ain't that man no more. *(He coughs up blood.)*

DONA ELENA. Oh, how it breaks my heart to see you so disappointed, *Cucaracha*. But revenge tastes sweetest when sprinkled with tears.

UNDERTAKER-BARBER. We're going to be rich!

DONA ELENA. Shut up! *(To HURACAN.)* Get me that suitcase, boy!

HURACAN. No!

EL NEGRO. Do as she says.

HURACAN. It ain't right. It belongs to you.

EL NEGRO. I don't want it no more. Too many ghosts.

UNDERTAKER-BARBER *(to DONA ELENA)*. Ghosts?

HURACAN. Yeah, ghosts... *(HURACAN crosses to pick up the suitcase.)* And devils too! *(He suddenly throws*

*the suitcase at the UNDERTAKER-BARBER scaring him
away. HURACAN howls.)*

UNDERTAKER-BARBER. Ay, *que susto! El Diablo!*

DONA ELENA. Come back, *idiota!*

*(The UNDERTAKER-BARBER runs off. HURACAN
chases after him. DONA ELENA picks up the shovel.)*

DONA ELENA. Coward! Just like your father! I should've
done this myself long ago!

EL NEGRO. Whatcha doin'?

DONA ELENA. Taking what belongs to me! I'll have it
all! *(She scoops up hot coals from the fire.)*

EL NEGRO. No, you can't do that!

DONA ELENA. Watch me! *(She throws the hot coals onto
the trees.)*

EL NEGRO. You settin' the trees on fire!

DONA ELENA. No one cheats me!

EL NEGRO. The whole forest is gonna burn!

HURACAN *(entering)*. No! *(HURACAN charges DONA
ELENA trying to stop her but she holds the shovel
threateningly.)*

DONA ELENA. Not so fast, *amigito!*

EL NEGRO *(weakened)*. I gotta save them monarchs! *(He
tries to stomp out the fire with a blanket.)*

DONA ELENA. You selfish boy! You had your chance! *(She
picks up the suitcase, but HURACAN grabs it at the
same time. They fight for it.)* Let go! It belongs to me!

HURACAN. No, it don't!

DONA ELENA. Let go before we all die!

(SOUND: A tree is heard exploding, startling DONA ELENA. She drops the suitcase.)

DONA ELENA *(exiting). Ay!* Go ahead and burn *El Negro.* Burn like those children! I'll see you in hell!

(EL NEGRO howls.)

EL NEGRO. Wake up, *mariposas!*

(HURACAN joins EL NEGRO howling.)

HURACAN. Fly *mariposas!* Fly!
EL NEGRO. Get up and fly away! Fly!

(SOUND: Another tree explodes.)

HURACAN. We got to get out of here!
EL NEGRO. No, leave me!
HURACAN. We gotta go! Now! *(He leads EL NEGRO out as the flames engulf the forest.)*

SCENE 12

"A chrysalis splits open and a new monarch emerges.— La crisálida se abre y brota una nueva mariposa monarca." La frontera—*Somewhere near the American border. A full moon. And two shadows appear.*

HURACAN *(singing)*.

> **Couldn't hear nobody pray**
> **Couldn't hear nobody pray** ...

EL NEGRO. Come on, old man!

HURACAN & EL NEGRO *(singing)*.

> **Oh, I'm just a way down yonder by myself**
> **And I couldn't hear nobody pray.**

(EL NEGRO falls to his knees. His breathing is labored.)

EL NEGRO. We in the states now. We through walkin'.

HURACAN. I thought there'd be fences, walls, men with guns and badges.

EL NEGRO. Not when we walk across. Gonna travel first class.

HURACAN *(proudly)*. I still got your suitcase.

EL NEGRO. I was hopin' you'd leave it. *(SOUND: A train whistle.)* There's our ride.

HURACAN. We ain't got no tickets.

EL NEGRO. Don't need none. We gonna ride hobo style. Now listen here, we got to be careful of them yard bulls.

HURACAN. Yard bulls?

EL NEGRO. They don't take to freeloaders on their trains. If they come chasin' after you, you run like hell. Them yard bulls carry guns and sticks. They ain't gonna ask questions.

HURACAN. When do we go?

EL NEGRO. What's you in such a hurry for?

HURACAN. I wanna get home. Find my *'amá* and my *'apá*.

EL NEGRO. We ain't goin' nowhere 'til that train moves. Hoboin' is about waitin'. Waitin' for the right moment. When that highball signals that's when we go. Gonna have to run fast and hard. Somewhere between the hog and crummy we gotta find ourselves an empty car.

HURACAN. Hog and crummy?

EL NEGRO. Hog's the locomotive. Crummy's the caboose. Highball is the whistle signalin' the train's leavin'. Do I gotta tell you everythin'?

HURACAN. Do you think them butterflies made it out?

EL NEGRO. Them monarchs got special magic. They fragile but they got a will to survive. They gonna be all right.

HURACAN. Like us?

EL NEGRO. That's right.

HURACAN. Them children ...

EL NEGRO. What children? ... Oh ... I never meant to hurt them children but I did. I carry their cries wherever I go. And there ain't day that goes by but I don't wish it was me in that house instead of them. I'm sorry, boy. I'm sorry for all the bad I done.

HURACAN. You think them children went to heaven?

EL NEGRO. I don't know.

HURACAN. I bet they did.

EL NEGRO. How do you figure?

HURACAN. Well, them monarch butterflies could've carried their souls up to heaven. And if they in heaven then their souls must be angels.

EL NEGRO. Angels?

HURACAN. And if they's angels then they can forgive.

EL NEGRO. Why would they forgive me?

HURACAN. 'Cause your butterflies carried them there.

EL NEGRO. You really believe that? *(SOUND: A train whistle is heard. EL NEGRO coughs.)* It's time for you to go!

HURACAN. Ain't you comin'?

EL NEGRO. I'll only hold you up. Go!

HURACAN. I ain't leavin' without you!

EL NEGRO. You gonna miss your train!

HURACAN. I ain't leavin' you!

EL NEGRO. Why you gotta argue with me?

HURACAN. 'Cause you a *cabezon!*

EL NEGRO. *Cabezon?*

HURACAN. That's right!

EL NEGRO. Wait 'til I get my hands on you!

HURACAN. Gotta catch me first, *cabezon! Cabezon!*

(EL NEGRO chases after HURACAN. They exit.)

SCENE 13

"The monarchs search for home.—Las mariposas monarcas buscan su hogar." *Lights flicker as the train rumbles through the desert. HURACAN and EL NEGRO are
in a boxcar. EL NEGRO lies on the floor. His breathing
is heavy. HURACAN holds the suitcase. EL NEGRO inhales the night air.*

HURACAN. What are you doing, old man?

EL NEGRO. It smells sweet, don't it?

HURACAN. What does?

EL NEGRO. Gringoland. *(He coughs. HURACAN inhales
the air.)*

HURACAN. We ridin' through the night, hobo style.

EL NEGRO. There ain't no borders for butterflies.

HURACAN & EL NEGRO. We's butterflies.

HURACAN. How much longer is it gonna take?

EL NEGRO. If we lucky. Couple more days.

(Something stirs in the boxcar. HURACAN picks up a stick.)

HURACAN. Who's there?
EL NEGRO. Be careful.

(TWO HOBOES step out of the shadows, It is a husband and wife. They are the same actors who played KIKA and MOISES.)

HUSBAND. Forgive us, *Señores*, we mean you no harm. My wife and I are hungry. Do you have anything to eat?
HURACAN. We got plenty. *(EL NEGRO starts to laugh.)* What's you laughing at, old man?
EL NEGRO. You a walkin' grocery store! You'll never go hungry.
HURACAN. That's right, I've learned. *(He gives the HUSBAND and WIFE some food.)*
WIFE. Thank you. *(HURACAN stares at the WIFE for a moment.)* What is it?
HURACAN. You remind me of someone.
WIFE. Who?
HURACAN. Someone I once knew.

(EL NEGRO coughs deeply. The WIFE touches EL NEGRO's face.)

HUSBAND. *El Señor* looks very ill.
HURACAN. He's gonna be all right.
WIFE. He has a fever.

HURACAN. No, he's just tired. That's all.

(The HUSBAND takes his blanket and places it on EL NEGRO.)

EL NEGRO. My lungs feel like they on fire. *(To the HUS-BAND.)* Who are you?

HUSBAND. My name is *Gabriel*. This is my wife, *Esperanza*.

WIFE. *Hola.*

EL NEGRO *(to HUSBAND)*. I seen you before. You from *Misas?*

HUSBAND. Oh, no, but I have lots of cousins there. We're heading north like you.

WIFE. Back to our home. We were sent away.

EL NEGRO. What's you got there?

HUSBAND. It's my *guitarra*. I can play something for you? Would *el Señor* like to hear something?

EL NEGRO. Play me somethin' sweet.

(The HUSBAND plays his guitar softly. A monarch butterfly gently floats into the boxcar and lands on HURACAN's hand.)

HURACAN. Where did you come from, little fella? Lookin' for a free ride, huh? Hobo butterfly. You can rest here all you want. *(EL NEGRO coughs.)* We almost home.

SCENE 14

"The monarch butterfly returns.—La mariposa monarca regresa." *HURACAN enters carrying EL NEGRO.*

EL NEGRO. Gotta catch my breath.
HURACAN *(singing)*.
  Roll, Jordan, roll; roll, Jordan, roll—
EL NEGRO. Put me down.
HURACAN *(singing)*.
  I want to go to heaven when I die,
  To hear ole' Jordan roll.
EL NEGRO. Please.
HURACAN. All right. But just for a while. *(He places EL NEGRO on the ground.)*
EL NEGRO. How come you in such a hurry?
HURACAN. I just am.
EL NEGRO. What's so special about today?
HURACAN. It's my birthday. I'll never be twelve again.

*(*El valle—*The valley. A barn sitting on the edge of a green field appears.)*

HURACAN *(discovering)*. We're here. Home. *(He searches.)* *'Amá? 'Apá? 'Amá?*
EL NEGRO. They ain't here?
HURACAN. *'Amá? 'Apá?*
EL NEGRO. I'm sorry, boy.
HURACAN. Maybe they waitin' somewhere else for me.
EL NEGRO. Maybe...
HURACAN. Maybe I gotta just keep lookin'.
EL NEGRO. Maybe. *(He coughs deeply.)*

HURACAN *(panicked)*. I can't do this alone. You gotta help me!

EL NEGRO. You gonna be fine, boy.

HURACAN. How do you know?

EL NEGRO. 'Cause I just do.

HURACAN. That's what my *'amá* once said and she never came back. *(EL NEGRO coughs deeply.)* Don't you quit on me, old man!

EL NEGRO *(proudly)*. My name's Benjamin Price.

(HURACAN opens EL NEGRO's hand and places some dirt in it.)

HURACAN. This is dirt, Benjamin Price. You hold it tight. This is gonna be our home.

EL NEGRO. Home. *(Coughs deeply.)*

HURACAN. Promise me you ain't gonna give up?

EL NEGRO. Do you see them?

HURACAN. See what?

EL NEGRO. Them monarchs!

HURACAN *(looks around, but there are no monarchs)*. I don't see anythin'.

EL NEGRO. Sure you do.

HURACAN. Where are they?

EL NEGRO. They all around you. Do you think they comin' for me?

HURACAN. "Don't walk away from a fight!" Remember your code!

EL NEGRO. So this is where they come to?

HURACAN. "Man's gotta pull his own weight!"

EL NEGRO. Look at them, circlin' all around me!

HURACAN. Get angry and fight!

EL NEGRO. There must be thousands of 'em.

HURACAN. Fight.

EL NEGRO. Ain't that a beautiful sight?

HURACAN. Please don't leave me!

EL NEGRO. Don't you see 'em? Don't you see 'em, son? *(Coughs deeply.)*

HURACAN. Yeah, I see 'em. Maybe we gotta feed them hungry butterflies, huh?

EL NEGRO. I can feel them lifting me up!

HURACAN. Dampen the earth with fresh water so the flowers will be strong.

EL NEGRO. They carryin' me up over the trees.

HURACAN. Feed them *mariposas* sweet nectar.

EL NEGRO. Up mountains. Past clouds.

HURACAN. A glimpse at God's heart.

EL NEGRO. To the highest heaven.

HURACAN. Fly! Benjamin Price. Fly!

EL NEGRO *(laughs)*. It tickles... *(He dies.)*

HURACAN. Benjamin Price?

(SOUND: The Negro spiritual heard at the opening of the play is introduced once again. HURACAN covers EL NEGRO with a blanket. He crosses to EL NEGRO's suitcase and opens it. It glows brightly. He smiles as hundreds of monarch butterflies emerge from it fluttering everywhere. HURACAN closes the suitcase. He picks it up and looks off into the horizon.)

HURACAN. I can do it. I can do it.

("The journey begins.—El viaje venturoso comienza.")

END OF PLAY

Glossary

Andale: Go on!

'Amá: Mother.

Amigito: Little friend.

'Apá: Father.

Ay, que susto!: Oh, what fright!

Cabezon: Knucklehead, hardheaded.

Chocolate: Chocolate candy.

Cucaracha: Cockroach.

Conejo: Rabbit.

Dia de los muertos: Day of the Dead: A holiday which blends the pre-Hispanic Aztec beliefs honoring the dead with the Catholic Church's All Saints' and All Souls' Days (November 1 and 2).

Deportados: Those who are deported.

El Diablo: The Devil.

Gringo: A North American citizen.

Guitarra: Guitar.

Idiota: Idiot.

Imposible: Impossible.

Indio: Indian.

La Llorona: The Weeping Woman. A legend having this ghostly woman wandering along canals and rivers crying for her missing children. Told to frighten children into behaving.

Mariposa: Butterfly.

Mijo: My son.

Monarca: Monarch butterfly.

Muchacho: Boy.

Nana: Grandmother.

No hay de que: You're welcome; don't mention it.

Sit Down Servant, Sit Down

Arranged by Darrell Louis Morgan
As sung by Lucille M. Oliver

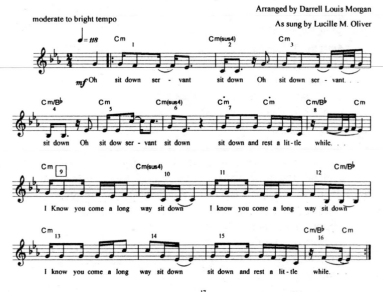

possible hand clap
rhythm for gospel
holy ghost feel

Hush, Somebody's Callin' My Name

As sung by Lucille M. Oliver
Arranged by Darrell Louis Morgan

Couldn't Hear Nobody Pray

As sung by Lucille M. Oliver

Arranged by Darrell Lewis Morgan

Roll Jordan Roll

Arranged by Darrell Louis Morgan

DIRECTOR'S NOTES

DIRECTOR'S NOTES

DIRECTOR'S NOTES